ANDREW LLOYD WEBBER™ for Ukulele

ISBN 978-1-4768-7449-4

HAL•LEONARD® CORPORATION

7777 W. BLUEMOUND RD. P.O. BOX 13819 MILWAUKEE, WI 53213

Visit Hal Leonard Online at
www.halleonard.com

All I Ask of You

from THE PHANTOM OF THE OPERA
Music by Andrew Lloyd Webber
Lyrics by Charles Hart
Additional Lyrics by Richard Stilgoe

Verse
Andante

Raoul:

1. No more talk of dark-ness, for-get these wide-eyed fears: I'm

here, noth-ing can harm you, my words will warm and calm you.

Let me be your free-dom, let day-light dry your tears: I'm

Chorus

here, with you, be-side you, to guard you and to guide you.

Christine:

Say you love me ev-ery

wak-ing mo-ment, turn my head with talk of sum-mer-time.

Chorus

Raoul:

say you'll share with me one love, one life - time; let me lead you from your

sol - i - tude. __ Say you need me with you, here be - side you,

an - y - where __ you go, let me go too. Chris - tine, __ that's all I ask of

Chorus

Christine:

Say you'll share with me one love, one life - time; say the word and I will
you.

fol - low you. __ Share each day with me, each night, each morn - ing.

Christine:

Say you love me!

Raoul:

You know I do.

Interlude

Both: *molto rit.* *a tempo*

Love me, that's all I ask of you.

(Instrumental)

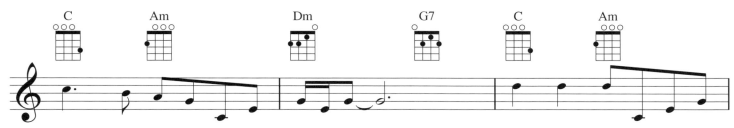

Outro

largo

An - y - where _ you go, let me go too;

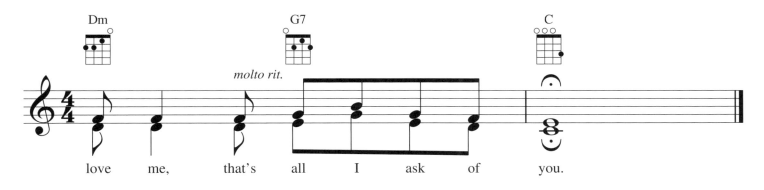

molto rit.

love me, that's all I ask of you.

Angel of Music

from THE PHANTOM OF THE OPERA
Music by Andrew Lloyd Webber
Lyrics by Charles Hart
Additional Lyrics by Richard Stilgoe

Now as I sing, I can sense him _____ and I know he's
Chris - tine, you're talk - ing in rid - dles, _____ and it's not like

1. E
here.

2. E
you.

Chorus

C: An - gel of mu - sic,

guide and guard - ian, grant to me your glo - ry! _____
(Who is this an - gel, this

An - gel of mu - sic, hide no long - er,
an - gel of mu - sic? Hide no long - er,

se - cret and strange an - gel. _____ *C:* He's
se - cret and strange an - gel.) _____

Bridge

with me e - ven now, all a - round me.

M: Your hands are cold. Your

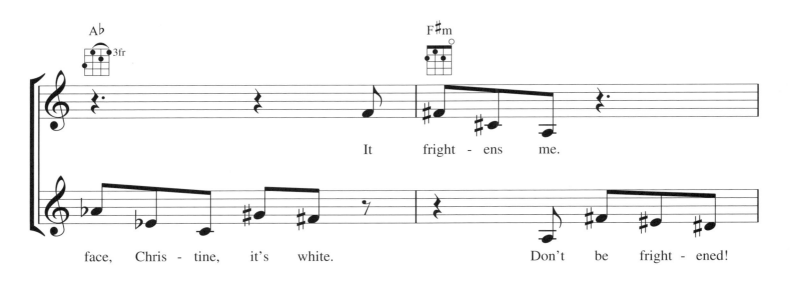

It fright - ens me.

face, Chris - tine, it's white. Don't be fright - ened!

Verse

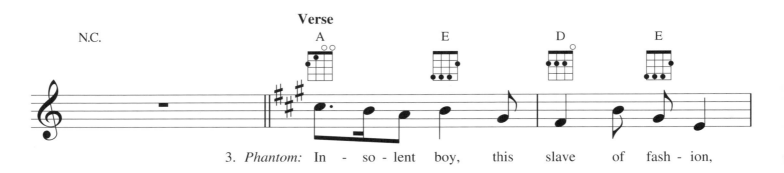

3. *Phantom:* In - so - lent boy, this slave of fash - ion,

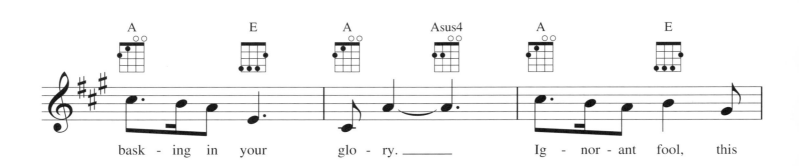

bask - ing in your glo - ry. _____ Ig - nor - ant fool, this

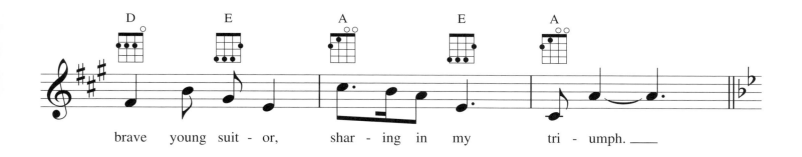

brave young suit - or, shar - ing in my tri - umph. ____

Verse

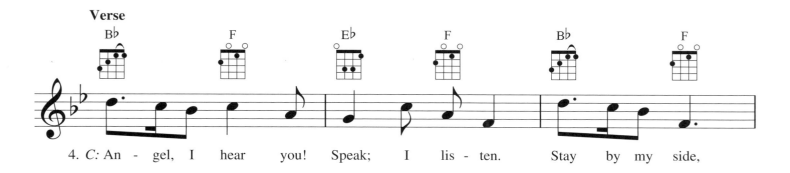

4. *C:* An - gel, I hear you! Speak; I lis - ten. Stay by my side,

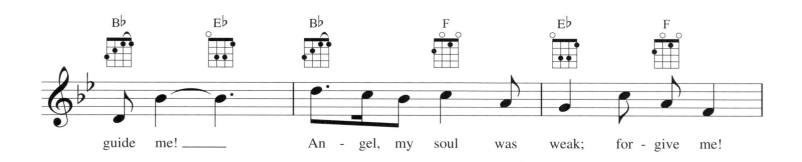

guide me! _____ An - gel, my soul was weak; for - give me!

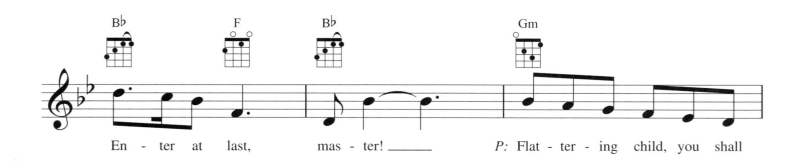

En - ter at last, mas - ter! _____ *P:* Flat - ter - ing child, you shall

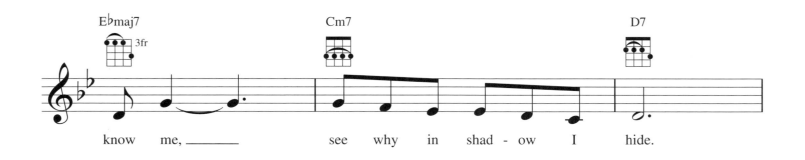

know me, _____ see why in shad - ow I hide.

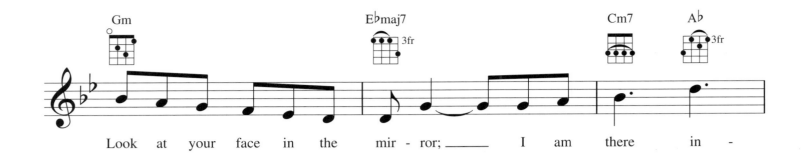

Look at your face in the mir - ror; ____ I am there in -

Chorus

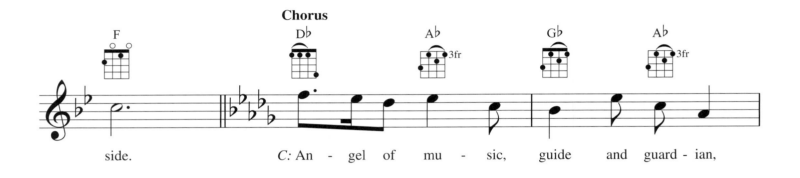

side.   C: An - gel of mu - sic, guide and guard - ian,

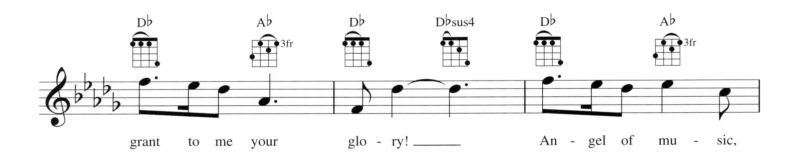

grant to me your glo - ry! ____ An - gel of mu - sic,

hide no long - er! Come to me, strange an - gel! ____

Close Every Door

from JOSEPH AND THE AMAZING TECHNICOLOR®DREAMCOAT
Music by Andrew Lloyd Webber
Lyrics by Tim Rice

bar all the win - dows and shut out the light.

La la la la la la, la la la la la la, la la la la la la,

la la la la la la, la la la la la la, la la la la la la,

la la la la la la, la. *(Instrumental)*

D.C. al Coda

Joseph: 2. Just

Coda

rit.

opt.

land ___ of our own.

Any Dream Will Do

from JOSEPH AND THE AMAZING TECHNICOLOR®DREAMCOAT
Music by Andrew Lloyd Webber
Lyrics by Tim Rice

gold - en   coat   flew   out   of   sight. __   The   col - ours   fad - ed

in - to   dark - ness,   I   was   left   a - lone. _____

3. May   I   re - turn   to   the   be -

gin - ning,   the   light   is   dim - ming   and   the   dream   is

too.   The   world   and   I,   we   are   still   wait - ing,

still   hes - i - tat - ing,   an - y   dream   will   do,

an - y   dream   will   do,   an - y   dream   will   do.

15

Buenos Aires

from EVITA
Words by Tim Rice
Music by Andrew Lloyd Webber

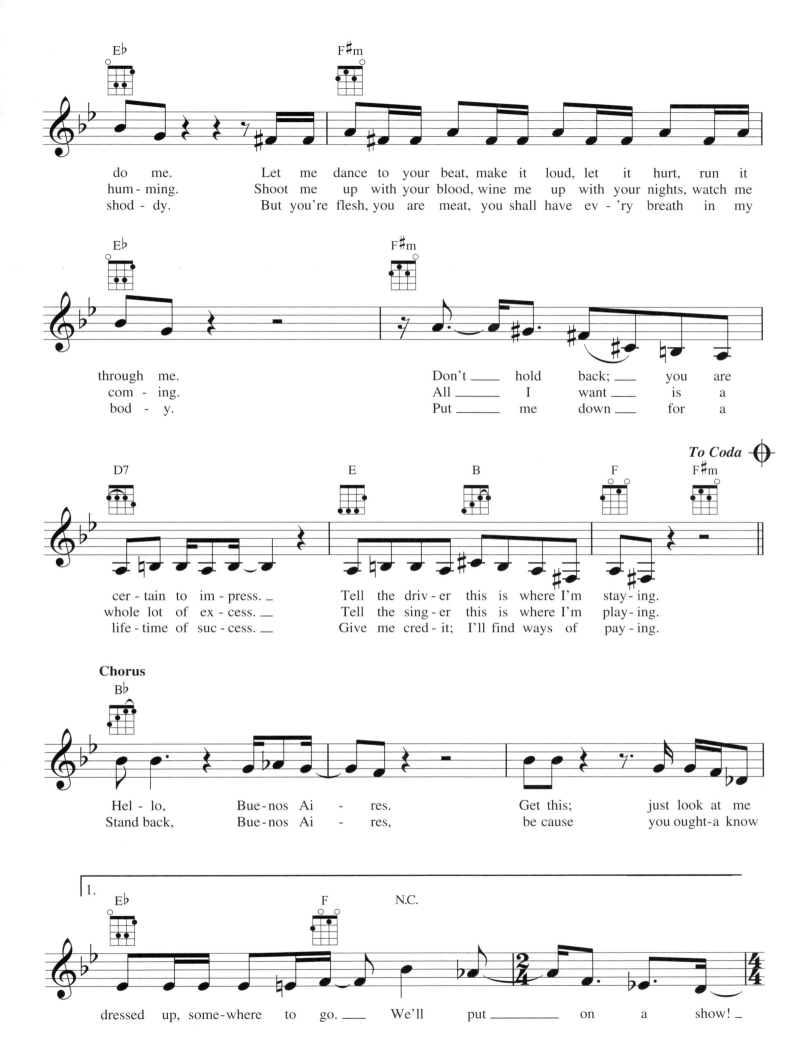

do me.   Let   me   dance to your beat, make it loud, let   it   hurt, run it
hum - ming.   Shoot me   up with your blood, wine me   up with your nights, watch me
shod - dy.   But you're flesh, you are meat, you shall have ev - 'ry breath in my

through me.   Don't ____ hold   back; ____ you   are
com - ing.   All ____   I   want ____ is   a
bod - y.   Put ____   me   down ____ for   a

To Coda ⊕

cer - tain to im - press. _   Tell the driv - er this is where I'm stay - ing.
whole lot of ex - cess. _   Tell the sing - er this is where I'm play - ing.
life - time of suc - cess. _   Give me cred - it; I'll find ways of pay - ing.

Chorus

Hel - lo,   Bue - nos Ai   -   res.   Get this;   just look at me
Stand back,   Bue - nos Ai   -   res,   be cause   you ought - a know

|1.

dressed up, some - where to go. ___ We'll put ____ on   a   show! _

2. Take me whatcha gon-na get in me: ___ just a

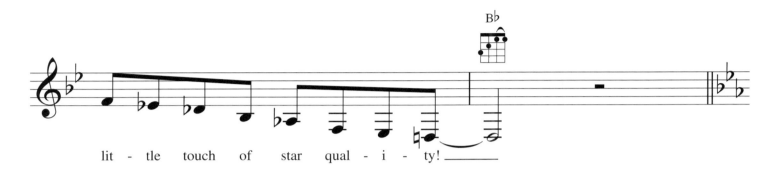

lit - tle touch of star qual - i - ty! _____

Bridge

And _____ if ev - er I go too far, ___
And _____ if I need a mo - ment's rest, ___

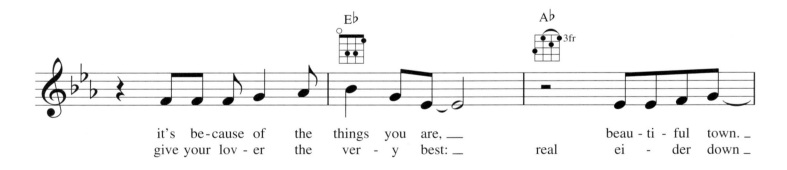

it's be-cause of the things you are, ___ beau - ti - ful town. _
give your lov - er the ver - y best: _ real ei - der down _

D.S. al Coda

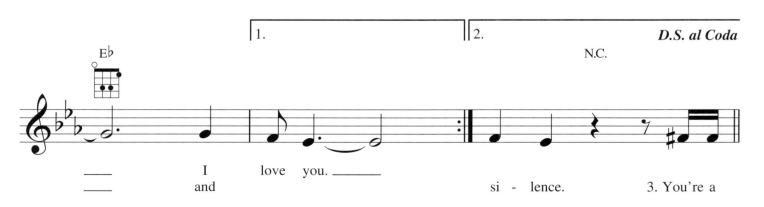

___ I love you. _____
___ and   si - lence.   3. You're a

Ri - o de la Pla - ta! Flo - ri - da! Cor - ri - en - tes!

Nu - e - ve de Ju - li - o! ____ All __ I _____ want to know. ____

Stand back, Bue - nos Ai - res, be - cause you ought - a know

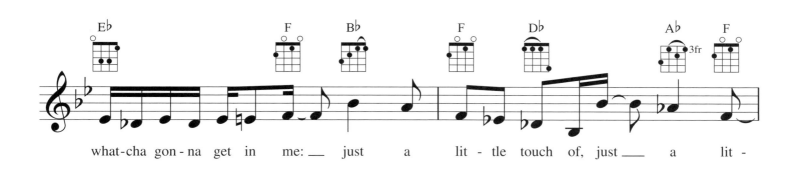

what - cha gon - na get in me: __ just a lit - tle touch of, just __ a lit -

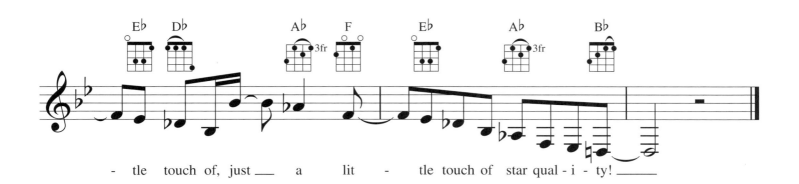

- tle touch of, just __ a lit - tle touch of star qual - i - ty! _____

Don't Cry for Me Argentina

from EVITA
Words by Tim Rice
Music by Andrew Lloyd Webber

Additional Lyrics

2. I had to let it happen, I had to change;
   Couldn't stay all my life down at heel,
   Looking out of the window, staying out of the sun.
   So I chose freedom, running around trying everything new,
   But nothing impressed me at all. I never expected it to.

3. And as for fortune and as for fame,
   I never invited them in,
   Though it seemed to the world they were all I desired.
   They are illusions, they're not the solutions they promised to be.
   The answer was here all the time. I love you and hope you love me.

The Music of the Night

from THE PHANTOM OF THE OPERA
Music by Andrew Lloyd Webber
Lyrics by Charles Hart
Additional Lyrics by Richard Stilgoe

First note

Verse
Moderately slow

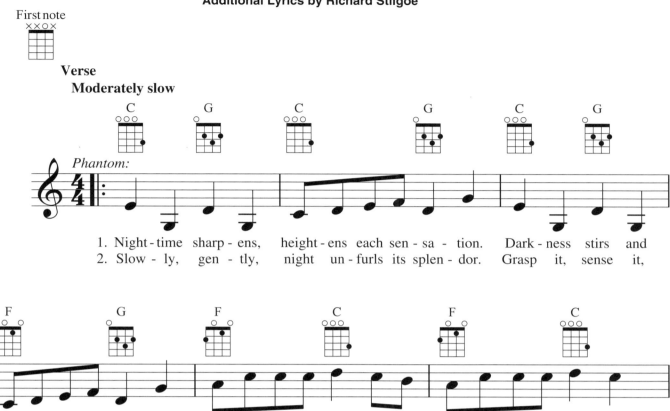

Phantom:

1. Night - time sharp - ens, height - ens each sen - sa - tion. Dark - ness stirs and
2. Slow - ly, gen - tly, night un - furls its splen - dor. Grasp it, sense it,

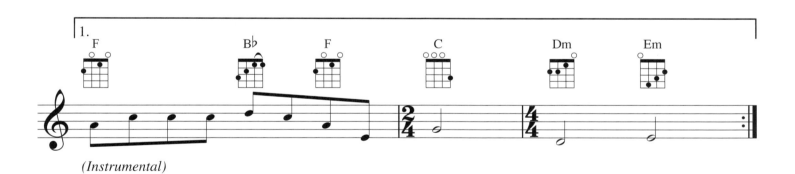

wakes i - mag - i - na - tion. Si - lent - ly the sens - es a - ban - don their de - fens - es.
trem - u - lous and ten - der. Turn your face a - way from the gar - ish light of day, turn your

1.

(Instrumental)

2.

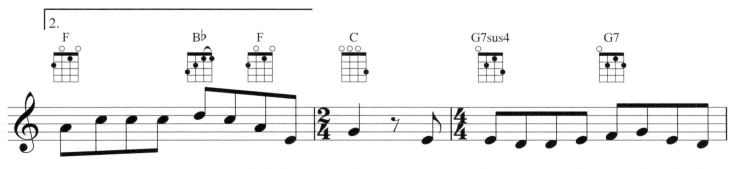

thoughts a - way from cold, un - feel - ing light and lis - ten to the mu - sic of the

Bridge

C   Bb

night.   Close   your   eyes   and   sur - ren - der   to   your
                     mind   start   a   jour - ney   through   a

Eb   Ab 3fr

dark - est   dreams.   Purge   your   thoughts   of   the   life   you   knew   be -
strange   new   world.   Leave   all   thoughts   of   the   life   you   knew   be -

D   D7   G   G7

fore.   Close   your   eyes,   let   your   spir - it   start   to
fore.   Let   your   soul   take   you   where   you   long   to

C   Em   B

soar,   and   you'll   live   as   you've   nev - er   lived   be -
be;   on - ly   then   can   you   be - long   to

Verse

E   C   G   C   G

fore.   3. Soft - ly,   deft - ly,   mu - sic   shall   ca - ress   you.
me.   4. Float - ing,   fall - ing,   sweet   in - tox - i - ca - tion.

C   G   F   G

Hear   it,   feel   it,   se - cret - ly   pos - sess   you.
Touch   me,   trust   me,   sa - vor   each   sen - sa - tion.

O-pen up your mind, let your fan-ta-sies un-wind in this
Let the dream be-gin, let your dark-er side give in to the

dark-ness which you know you can-not fight, the dark-ness of the mu-sic of the
pow-er of the mu-sic that I write, the pow-er of the mu-sic of the

1.　　　　　　　　2.

Interlude

night.　　　Let your　night.
(Instrumental)

Outro

You a-lone can make my song take flight.　　　Help me make the mu-sic of the

night. _____

25

Everything's Alright

from JESUS CHRIST SUPERSTAR
Words by Tim Rice
Music by Andrew Lloyd Webber

I Don't Know How to Love Him

from JESUS CHRIST SUPERSTAR
Words by Tim Rice
Music by Andrew Lloyd Webber

Learn to Be Lonely

from THE PHANTOM OF THE OPERA, THE MOVIE
Music by Andrew Lloyd Webber
Lyrics by Charles Hart

First note

Verse
Moderately, somewhat freely

Child of the wil-der-ness, born in-to emp-ti-ness, learn to be lone-ly, learn to find your way in dark-ness. Who will be there for you? Com-fort and care for you? Learn to be lone-ly, learn to be your

Bridge

one com-pan-ion. Nev-er dream that out in the world

there are arms to hold you. You've al - ways known your

Outro-Verse

heart was on its own. So laugh in your lone - li - ness,

child of the wil - der - ness. Learn to be lone - ly,

learn how to love life that is lived a - lone.

(Instrumental)

Outro

Learn to be

lone - ly. Life can be lived, life can be loved a - lone.

33

Memory

from CATS

Music by Andrew Lloyd Webber
Text by Trevor Nunn after T.S. Eliot

No Matter What

from WHISTLE DOWN THE WIND
Music by Andrew Lloyd Webber
Lyrics by Jim Steinman

First note

Verse
Moderately slow

1. No mat-ter what they tell us, no mat-ter what they
2. If on-ly tears were laugh-ter, if on-ly night was

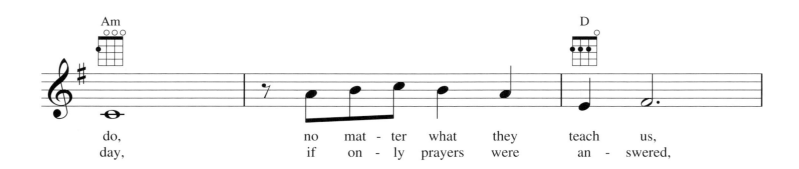

do, no mat-ter what they teach us,
day, if on-ly prayers were an-swered,

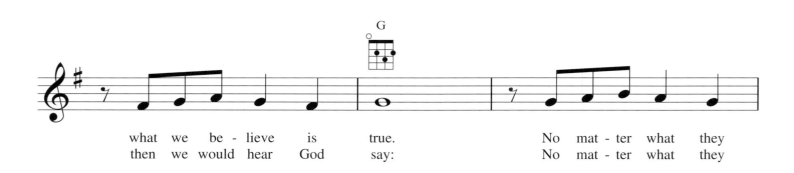

what we be-lieve is true. No mat-ter what they
then we would hear God say: No mat-ter what they

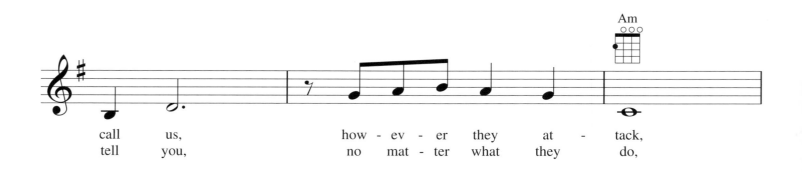

call us, how-ev-er they at-tack,
tell you, no mat-ter what they do,

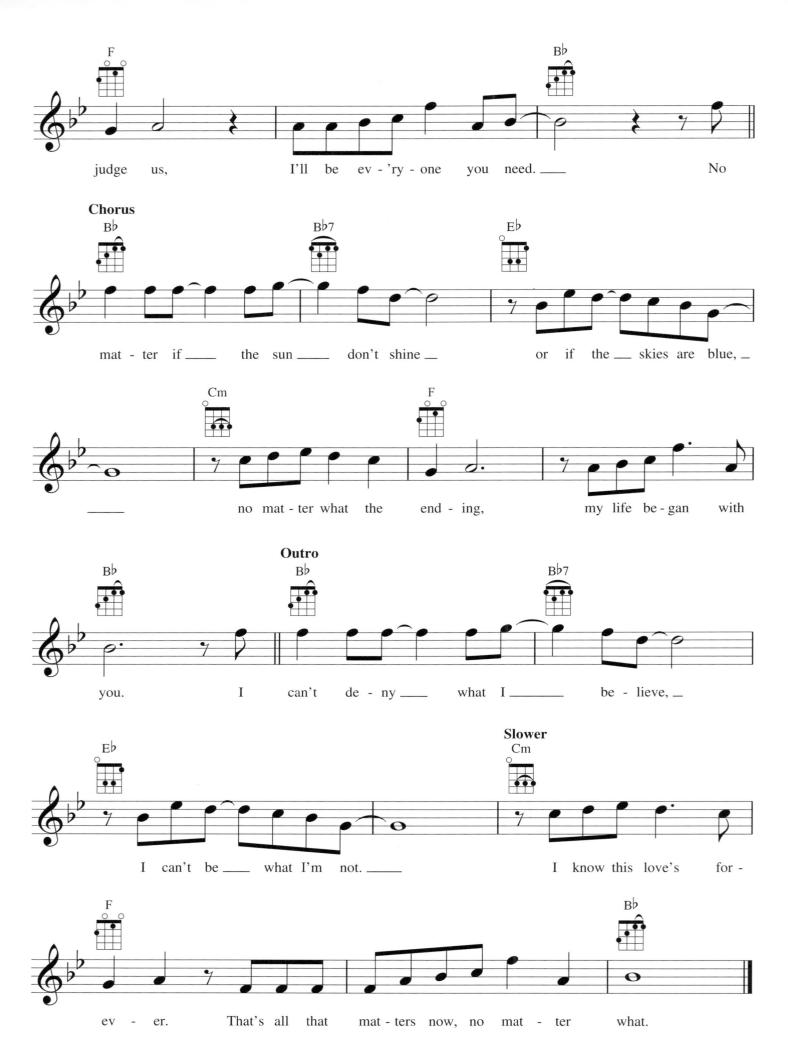

The Perfect Year

from SUNSET BOULEVARD
Music by Andrew Lloyd Webber
Lyrics by Don Black and Christopher Hampton

First note

Moderately

Verse

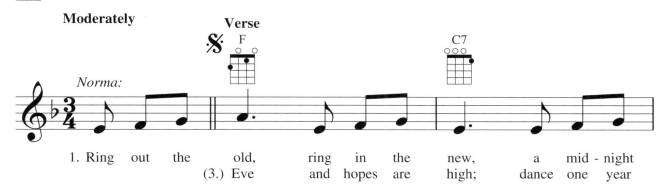

Norma:

1. Ring out the old, ring in the new, a mid-night
(3.) Eve and hopes are high; dance one year

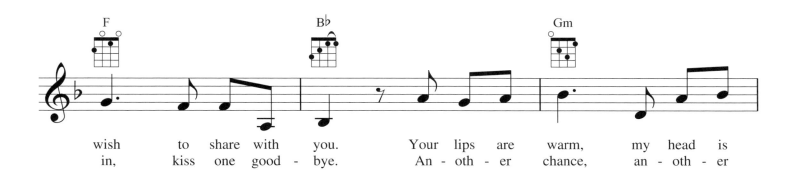

wish to share with you. Your lips are warm, my head is
in, kiss one good - bye. An - oth - er chance, an - oth - er

light; were we a - live be - fore to - night?
start, so man - y dreams to tease the heart.

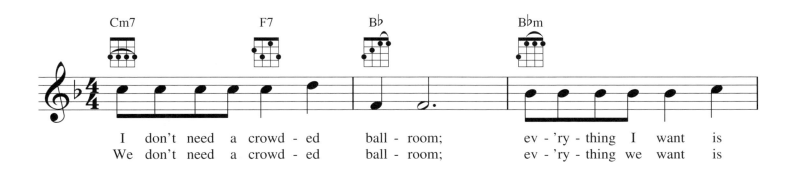

I don't need a crowd - ed ball - room; ev - 'ry - thing I want is
We don't need a crowd - ed ball - room; ev - 'ry - thing we want is

here.   If you're with   me, _____ next year will   be _____ the per - fect

here,   and face to   face _____ we will em - brace _____ the per - fect

Verse

year.   *Joe:* 2. Be - fore we   play _____ some dan - gerous game, _____ be - fore we

fan _____ some harm - less flame,   we have to   ask _____ if this is

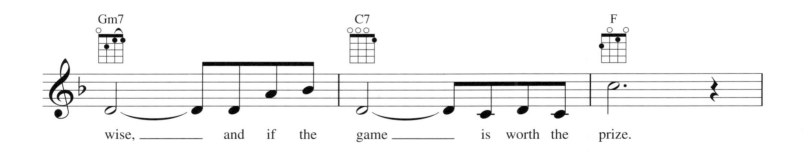

wise, _____ and if the   game _____ is worth the prize.

With this wine and with   this   mu - sic,   how can an - y - thing be

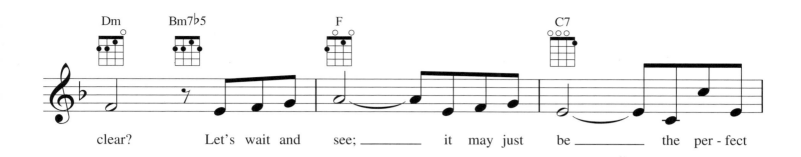

clear?   Let's wait and   see; _____ it may just be _____ the per - fect

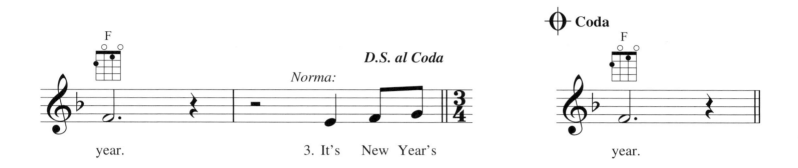

D.S. al Coda

⊕ **Coda**

Norma:

year.   3. It's   New   Year's   year.

Outro

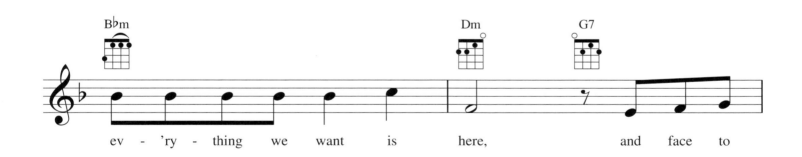

We   don't   need   a   crowd - ed   ball - room;

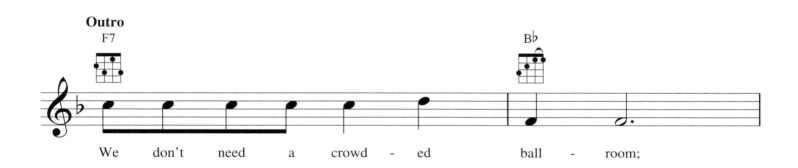

ev - 'ry - thing   we   want   is   here,   and   face   to

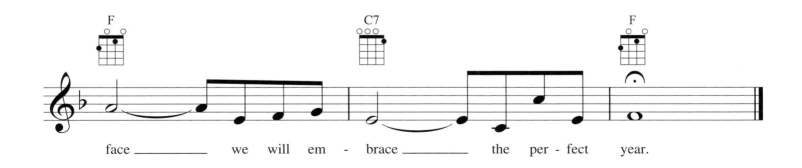

face _____ we   will   em - brace _____ the   per - fect   year.

The Phantom of the Opera

from THE PHANTOM OF THE OPERA
Music by Andrew Lloyd Webber
Lyrics by Charles Hart
Additional Lyrics by Richard Stilgoe and Mike Batt

Verse

Phantom: 4. In all your fan - ta - sies, _____

_____ you al - ways knew _____ that man and mys - ter - y _____

_____ *C:* were both in you.

{ *C:* And in this la - by - rinth _____
{ *P:* And in this la - by - rinth _____

_____ where night is blind, _____ the phan -
_____ where night is blind, _____ the phan -

- tom of the op - er - a is here _____ in - side my
- tom of the op - er - a is there _____ in - side your

mind. *Phantom: Sing, my angel of music!* *Christine:* He's
mind.

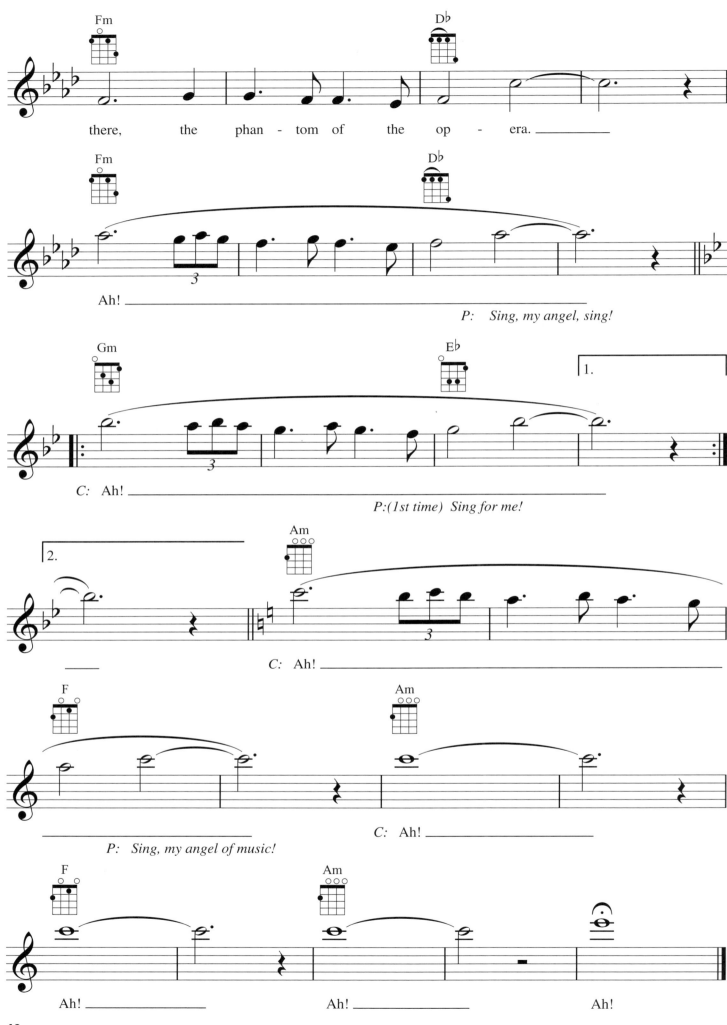

Take That Look Off Your Face

from TELL ME ON A SUNDAY

Music by Andrew Lloyd Webber
Lyrics by Don Black

Superstar

from JESUS CHRIST SUPERSTAR
Words by Tim Rice
Music by Andrew Lloyd Webber

First note

Verse
Lively Rock

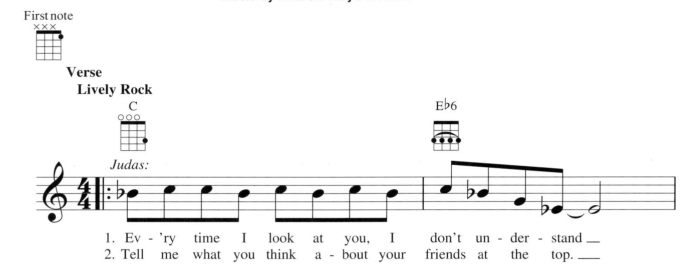

1. Ev - 'ry time I look at you, I don't un - der - stand ___
2. Tell me what you think a - bout your friends at the top. ___

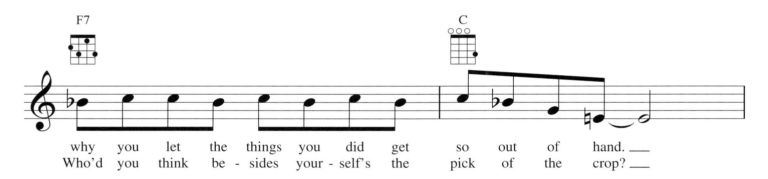

why you let the things you did get so out of hand. ___
Who'd you think be - sides your - self's the pick of the crop? ___

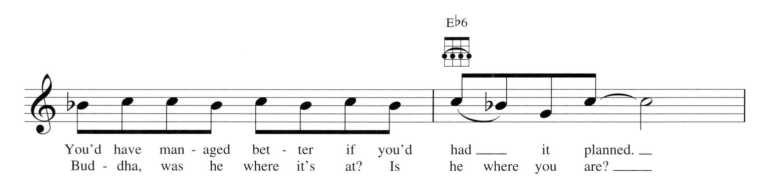

You'd have man - aged bet - ter if you'd had ___ it planned. ___
Bud - dha, was he where it's at? Is he where you are? _____

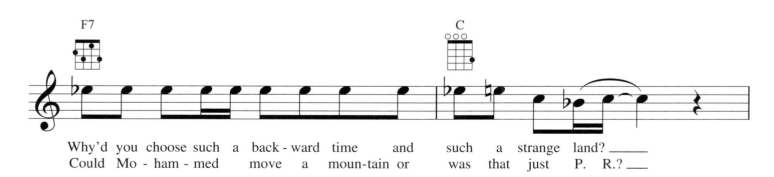

Why'd you choose such a back - ward time and such a strange land? ___
Could Mo - ham - med move a moun - tain or was that just P. R.? ___

If you'd come to - day, you would have reached a whole na - tion.
Did you mean to die like that? Was that a mis - take, ___ or

Is - rael in Four B. C. had no mass com - mu - ni - ca - tion.)
did you know your mess - y death would be a rec - ord break - er?

Choir:
(Don't you get me

wrong.) (Don't you get me wrong, now.) (Don't you get me
Don't you get me wrong. _ Don't you get me wrong. _

wrong.) (Don't you get me wrong, now.) (I on - ly want to
Don't you get me wrong. _ Don't you get me wrong. _

know.) (I on - ly want to know, now.) (I on - ly want to
On - ly want to know. _ On - ly want to know. _

know.)   (I on - ly want to   know, now.)
On - ly want to know. __   On - ly want to   know. __

Chorus

Je - sus Christ, __   Je - sus Christ. __   Who are you? What have you

sac - ri - ficed? __   Je - sus Christ, __   Je - sus Christ. __

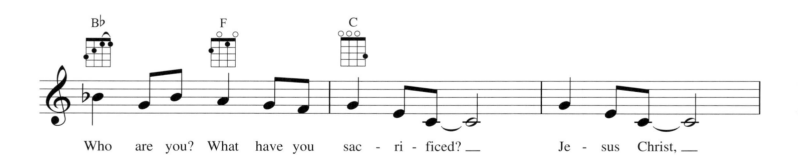

Who are you? What have you   sac - ri - ficed? __   Je - sus Christ, __

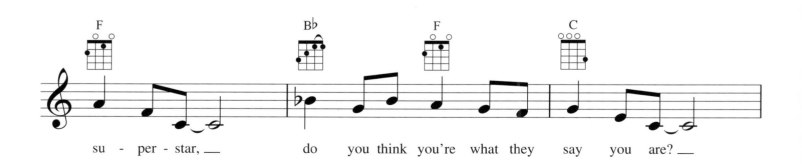

su - per - star, __   do you think you're what they say you are? __

52

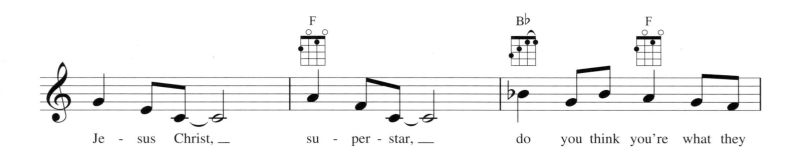

Je - sus Christ, __ su - per - star, __ do you think you're what they

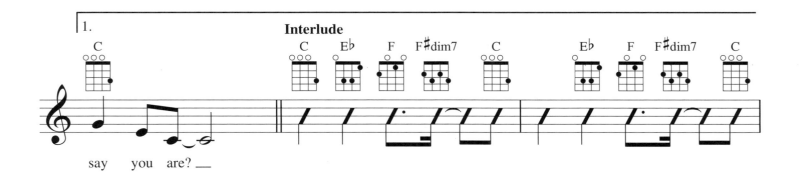

1. **Interlude**

say you are? __

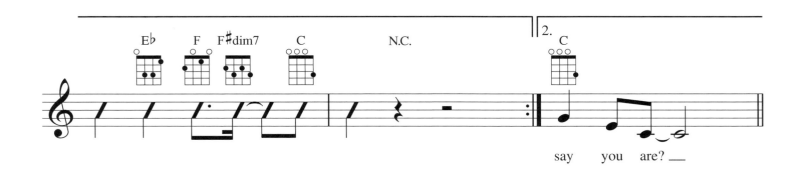

2.

N.C.

say you are? __

Outro

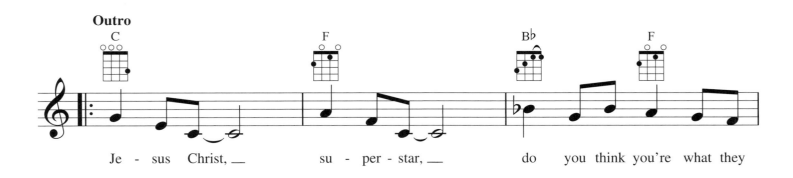

Je - sus Christ, __ su - per - star, __ do you think you're what they

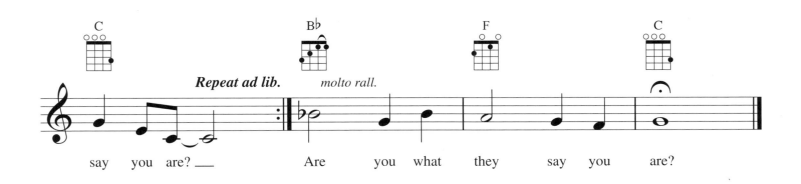

Repeat ad lib. *molto rall.*

say you are? __ Are you what they say you are?

Think of Me

from THE PHANTOM OF THE OPERA
Music by Andrew Lloyd Webber
Lyrics by Charles Hart
Additional Lyrics by Richard Stilgoe

ev - er find a mo - ment,   spare a thought for
you can still re - mem - ber,   stop and think of
nev - er be a day when

me.   me.   Think of all the things we've shared and

seen;   don't think a - bout the things which might have been.

I won't think of you.
(Instrumental)

Raoul: 4. Can it be,   can it be Chris - tine?   *(Instrumental)*

What a change; _ you're real - ly not a bit _ the gawk - ish

girl that once you were. She may not re-mem-ber me, but

Outro

I re-mem-ber her.

Christine: We nev-er said ____ our love was

ev-er-green ____ or as un-chang-ing as the sea, but please

prom-ise me that some-times you will

think... ah _____ ah _____ ah ____

_____ ah _____ of me!

Wishing You Were Somehow Here Again

from THE PHANTOM OF THE OPERA
Music by Andrew Lloyd Webber
Lyrics by Charles Hart
Additional Lyrics by Richard Stilgoe

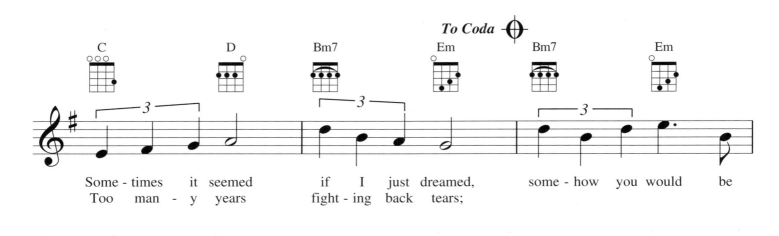

To Coda ⊕

Some - times it seemed if I just dreamed, some - how you would be
Too man - y years fight - ing back tears;

here. Wish - ing I could hear your voice a - gain,

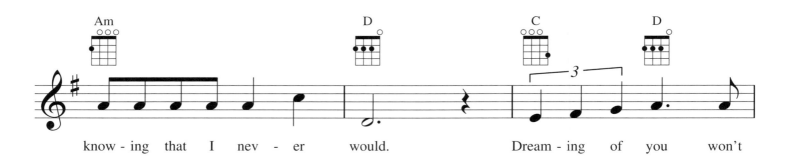

know - ing that I nev - er would. Dream - ing of you won't

D.C. al Coda

help me to do all that you dreamed I could.

⊕ **Coda**

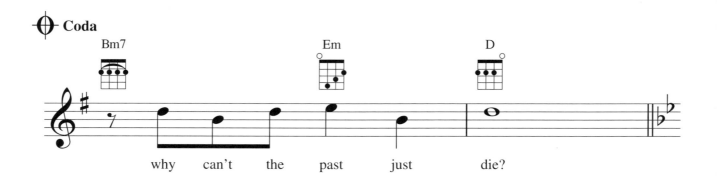

why can't the past just die?

Wish-ing you were some-how here a-gain, know-ing we must say good-

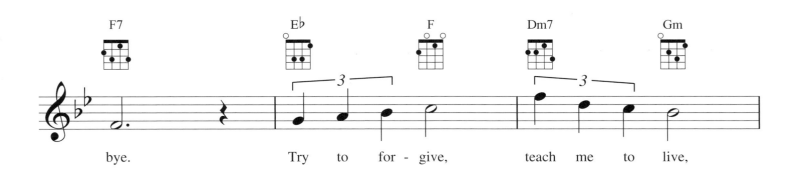

bye. Try to for-give, teach me to live,

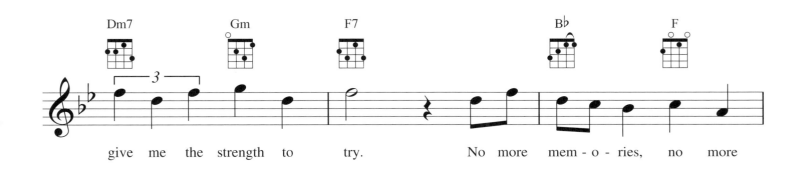

give me the strength to try. No more mem-o-ries, no more

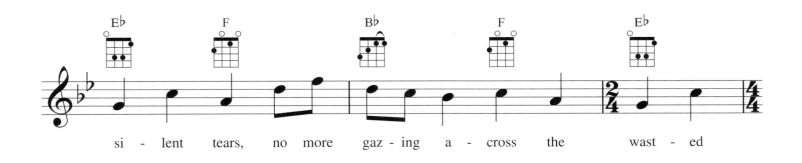

si-lent tears, no more gaz-ing a-cross the wast-ed

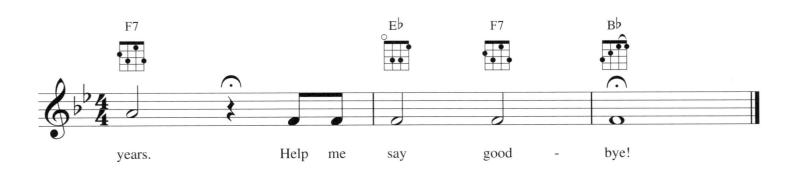

years. Help me say good-bye!

Whistle Down the Wind

from WHISTLE DOWN THE WIND

Music by Andrew Lloyd Webber
Lyrics by Jim Steinman

1. Whis-tle down the wind, _____ let your voic-es car-ry. _____
2. Howl _ at the stars, _____ whis-per when you're sleep-ing. _

Drown out all the rain, light a patch of dark-ness,
I'll be there to hold you, I'll be there to stop the

treach-er-ous and scar - y. _____
chills and all the weep - ing. __

Make it

Bridge

clear and strong _____ so the whole night long _ ev-'ry

sig-nal that you send, un-til the ver-y end I will not a-ban-don

Unexpected Song

from TELL ME ON A SUNDAY
Music by Andrew Lloyd Webber
Lyrics by Don Black

words,   your smile has real - ly thrown me.   This   is not like me at
all,   what - ev - er made you choose me?   I   just can't be - lieve my

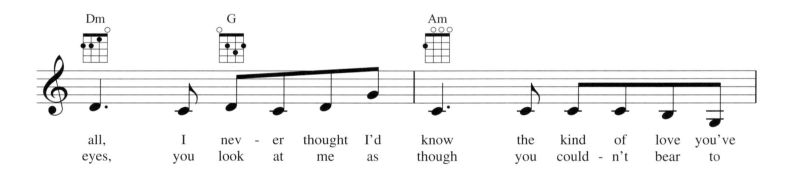

all,   I nev - er thought I'd know   the kind of love you've
eyes,   you look at me as though   you could - n't bear to

Chorus

shown me.
lose me.

Now,   no mat - ter where I am,   no mat - ter what I

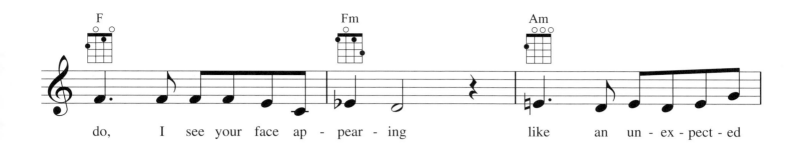

do,   I   see   your   face   ap - pear - ing   like   an   un - ex - pect - ed

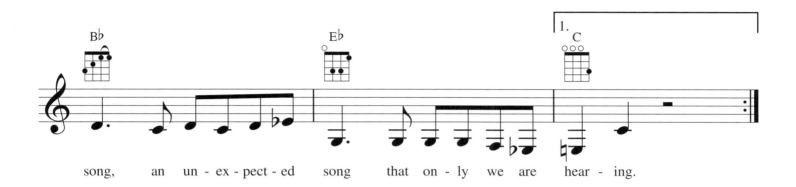

song,   an   un - ex - pect - ed   song   that   on - ly   we   are   hear - ing.

hear - ing.   3. I   have   nev - er   felt   like   this,   for once I'm   lost   for

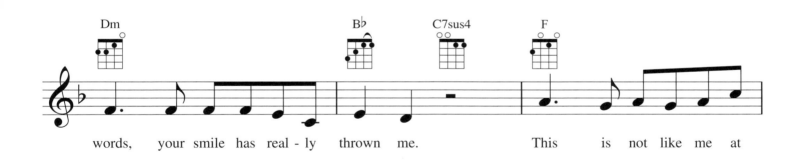

words,   your smile has   real - ly   thrown   me.   This   is   not   like   me   at

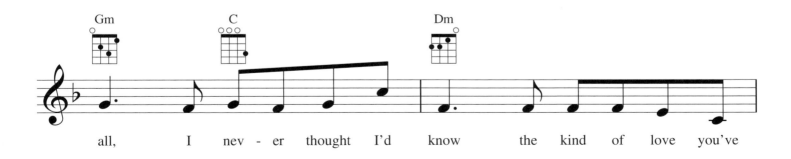

all,   I   nev - er   thought   I'd   know   the   kind   of   love   you've

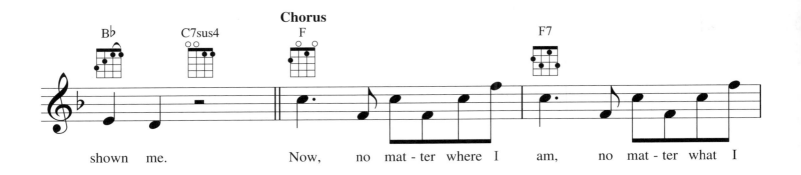

Chorus

shown me. Now, no mat - ter where I am, no mat - ter what I

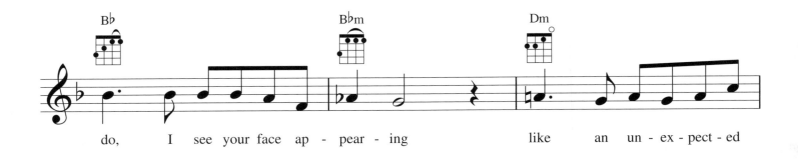

do, I see your face ap - pear - ing like an un - ex - pect - ed

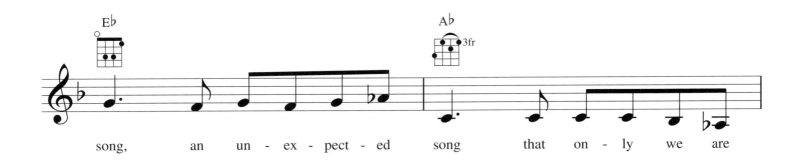

song, an un - ex - pect - ed song that on - ly we are

Outro

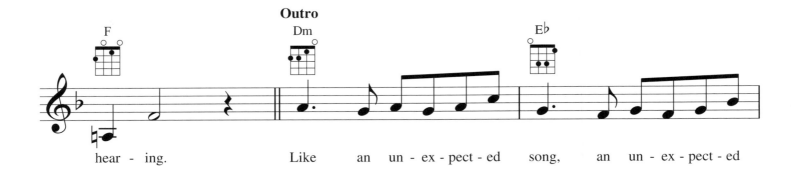

hear - ing. Like an un - ex - pect - ed song, an un - ex - pect - ed

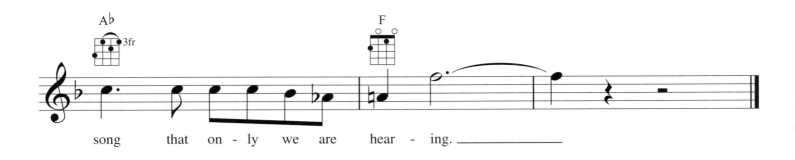

song that on - ly we are hear - ing. _____